God, Remember Me?

Rekindling the Flame in Your Relationship with God

14-Day Devotional

LAKECIA WILSON

God, Remember Me?

Copyright © 2020 by LaKecia Wilson.

Scripture quotations marked NKJV are from the New King James Version®. Copyright © 1982 by Thomas Nelson. Used by permission. All rights reserved.

Scripture quotations marked NLT are from the New Living Translation Version®. Copyright © 1996, 2004, 2007 by Tyndale House Foundation. Used by permission. All rights reserved.

Print ISBN: 9780974702025

Ebook ISBN: 9780974702018

Printed in the United States of America

DEDICATION

This book is dedicated to all of those who somewhere in their walk and relationship with God lost their passion and zeal in the relationship but truly want it back.

I also dedicate this book to my bestfriend, my sister in Christ, and my listening ear, Nicole Hardin. Thank you for always keeping it real with me and reminding me of who God called me to be. You keep me accountable to the call He placed on my life and don't allow or tolerate me to deter from it. I love you to pieces!

FOREWORD

If you have a desire to recommit your relationship with the Lord this is a must read. It is an honor and a privilege we have in knowing LaKecia Wilson. Minister Wilson possesses a selfless zeal for helping others become successful in the Lord. Her positive approach will both challenge and motivate you to reexamine your connection with God. Minister Wilson is committed to helping readers of all ages understand the correlation between faithfully implementing such truths, and living the abundant life that God has ordained for His people. Through relevant scripture references, she succinctly points out the road map for reestablishing a closer walk with God.

We are delighted to recommend this inspiring devotional to those desiring a shift in their commitment with the Lord. We thank God for your labor of love to the Body of Christ.

Overseer AJ and Pastor Angelique Monterio

Victory Worship Center
San Antonio, Texas

TABLE OF CONTENTS

INTRODUCTION

Does this sound familiar? You find yourself promising God that you will spend time with Him later that day because you're running late for work. Better yet, you tell yourself you don't have to get up early to spend time with Him because you'll have time to do it later. You haven't picked up your Bible in weeks and tell yourself one more day won't hurt. You promise you'll read it tomorrow.

Somewhere along the line, you stop putting forth the effort in your relationship with God. For some, you can't recall when or where it happened. You may not even be sure of what caused it. All you know is that one day you looked up and it had been weeks or months since you spent time with God.

You can't recall the last time you prayed a heartfelt prayer. Lately you've prayed quick prayers, sometimes all you could utter is "help me God." You looked up and can't recall when you genuinely studied the Word of God or sat in quiet to hear what the One Who loves you wanted to whisper to you.

You reminisce about how your relationship with God used to be, but you don't recall when it all changed. The guilt has set in and you don't know how to find your way back into those intimate moments with Him.

The devil starts whispering lies like "It's too late," "God isn't going to forgive you," "God has forgotten about you like you forgot about Him," or even "It's been too long." All lies! It's never too late to reconnect with God and reignite the relationship you once had.

You feel so distant from God that you wonder if He even remembers you. You find yourself asking, God, do you remember me? As if He could ever forget you, the one He formed in your mother's womb, the one who He knows the number of hairs on your head.

You may not know where you put your relationship with God down at or the exact moment you put it down, but the yearning is still there for that intimacy. If it wasn't, you wouldn't be feeling guilty about it and wanting it back.

When you get in the habit of not spending that intimate time with God, you look up one day and discover you've disconnected from Him and that relationship you once had with Him has fallen along the wayside.

The good news is that God remembers you and wants to spend time with you. He's waiting on you. You can reignite the passion in your relationship with God. It all starts with desire. That desire to be back in relationship with your Creator. That desire is what can rekindle the flame.

We've all been in relationships before, which is why I'll be using the analogy of a relationship to walk you through this 14-day devotional. This book is for those ready to rekindle the passionate and intimate relationship they once had with God. Take the next 14 days to rekindle the flame between you and God. He's been desiring your return. He misses you and He's ready and waiting for you. Are you ready?

God, Remember Me?

DAY ONE

Something Is Wrong

The first step in fixing a problem is admitting that there is a problem. Admitting you have a problem is not a sign of weakness. It's really a sign of strength. Are you strong enough to admit that there's something that's gone wrong in your relationship with God?

You look up one day and realize either your relationship with God is not the same or you're not even in relationship with Him anymore. You don't talk to Him as often as you used to. You don't put forth the effort to spend time with Him and it doesn't bother you that you don't. You don't feel guilty about being distant with Him. It's grown to feel normal. You sit back and realize it's not normal at all. It's the moment you realize something is wrong in your relationship and it needs to be fixed.

The next step is admitting you're the problem. When it comes to distance in our relationship with God, yes, we are the problem. It's never God. He's a relational God who desires intimacy with us. He's crazy about you even when you're not crazy about Him. He's in love with you even when you've pulled yourself away from Him. You're constantly on His mind when you're not even thinking of Him during those distant times.

Give thanks to the God of heaven.
His faithful love endures forever.
Psalm 136:26
New Living Translation (NLT)

Now that you realize you're not as close as you once were to God, what are you going to do about? You can keep going down the path you're going and continue to grow more distant to Him or you can draw toward Him. It doesn't matter how long it's been since you last talked to Him, listened to Him, prayed to Him, or studied His Word. He wants you back! He never stopped loving you. He never stopped waiting to hear from you. He not once left you. He wants you back! Just take that next step, a step towards Him. A step back into relationship with Him.

Draw near to God and He will draw near to you.
James 4:8
New King James Version (NKJV)

What do you think contributed to you growing distant from God?

How could you have acted (reacted) differently?

What could you have done differently?

How will you address this to ensure it (they) won't cause you to distance yourself again?

Prayer:

God, I realize I've grown distant in my relationship with You and that I miss You. I allowed _____ (name it or them) to cause me to not want to spend time with You. I'm sorry and I want to draw near back to You. I want those intimate moments back that we once shared.

Strengthen me and help me to come back into relationship with You. Help me to overcome what I allowed to put a wedge between us so that it doesn't happen again. I love You God and I miss you! Thank You for never giving up on me. In Jesus' name I pray. Amen.

DAY TWO
When Did It Go Wrong?

All of us remember some point in our lives when we were head over heels in love. You talked on the phone with the one you loved through the wee hours of the night. You just couldn't get enough of being around them. You wanted to spend any time you could with them. Just the thought of the took your breath away.

> *"Let me see your face;*
> *Me hear your voice.*
> *For your voice is pleasant,*
> *and your face is lovely.*
> *Song of Songs 2:14b*
> *New Living Translation (NLT)*

You were excited each day to either see them or talk to them. Every time you heard their voice, your heart pounded even harder. Each day brought something exciting, fresh and new into the relationship.

For some, after being together for a while, without intentionally doing it, you started to neglect one another. You didn't talk as much. You didn't spend as much time together. You found yourselves in the same room or house with barely anything to say to one another. The excitement was gone. The thrill was gone.

> *One night as I lay in bed, I yearned for*
> *my love. I yearned for him, but he did*
> *not come. So I said to myself, "I will get*
> *up and roam the city, searching in all*
> *its streets and squares.*
> *I will search for the one I love."*
> *So I searched everywhere but did not find him.*
> *Song of Songs 3:1-2*
> *New Living Translation (NLT)*

What happened? How did you get there? The same often happens with our relationship with God. We start off with so much zeal and passion. We look forward to spending time with Him and pondering over His Word. We wait in excitement and anticipation for Him to talk to us. Then one day we look up and we haven't had a conversation with Him in a while. We don't know the last time we studied the Word of God then patiently awaited to hear His voice. We find ourselves asking that oh too familiar question, "What happened?"

> *I opened to my lover,*
> *but he was gone!*
> *My heart sank.*
> *I searched for him*
> *but could not find him anywhere.*
> *I called to him,*
> *But there was no reply.*
> *Song of Songs 5:6*
> *New Living Translation (NLT)*

In any relationship where the passion fizzles out, you have to step back and ask yourself how you may have contributed to that. The same goes for our relationship with God. After all, He's not the one who pulled away. What contributed to your pulling away? You have to address the cause so you can deal with them and not allow them to cause a wedge between you and your Creator again. You don't want those issues creeping up and putting distance between you and God again.

When did you notice your relationship with God wasn't the same?

List some things (i.e., time, stress, etc.) that contributed to you spending less and less time with God on a daily basis.

What can you do differently to prevent these things from coming between you and God?

Prayer:

God, forgive me for pulling away from you. I allowed (time, stress, people/person, work, situations, etc.) come between us. I'm sincerely sorry and want to reconnect with You. Show me God how not to allow these things to separate us again. I acknowledge I need you daily. Daily, I need Your presence and Your Word. Show me how to balance this life I live and the time given to

me so I can spend time with You daily. I've missed You and I love You. I look forward to us reconnecting in an intimate relationship again. In Jesus' Name I pray. Amen.

Come away, my love!
Song of Songs 8:14a
New Living Translation (NLT)

DAY THREE

Something Between Us

If left unchecked, as time passes and there's no intimacy in your relationship, the distance grows more and more between you and that person. So, it is with your relationship with God. The more the time passes, the longer the distance becomes and one day you look up and see this giant "something" between the two of you. It appears so wide and so deep that you think you'll never find your way back to God.

What can I say about you?
Who has ever seen such sorrow?
O daughter of Jerusalem, to what can I
compare your anguish?
O virgin daughter of Zion, how can I
comfort you?
For your wound is as deep as the sea.

Who can heal you?
Lamentations 2:13
New Living Translation (NLT)

That "something" has made it seem like you don't love that person anymore. Whatever caused you to distance yourself from God has made it appear that you don't want to have anything to do with God anymore. After all, you haven't been talking to Him. You haven't desired to hear His voice. When He has tried to talk to you, you've ignored Him. You've had no desire to even pick up the Bible to read or study it. And fasting, well let's just say, you've haven't missed any food lately. It seems like you don't love Him or want to have anything to do with Him anymore, but know that the love is still there. While you may feel distant from Him, his love has lasted for you through it all.

I will never forget this awful time,
as I grieve over my loss.
Yet I still dare to hope when I
remember this: The faithful love of the
Lord never ends!

His mercies never cease.
Great is his faithfulness;
His mercies begin afresh each morning.
I say to myself, "The Lord is my
inheritance; therefore, I will hope in him!"
Lamentations 3:20-24
New Living Translation (NLT)

That "something" that's come between you and the one you love has caused so much distance between you that you feel uncomfortable and don't know what to do or even what to say to that person. You seem to can't find the peace, joy, or happiness you once had. You pause and realize just how much you miss the one you love. Now the question is how to fix what has happened? What do you say? What do you do? How do you say it? How do you do it? The answer to that is easy, "Just do it."

One of the most effective ways to remove the distance is by communicating what caused it. Let God know why you've been upset with Him or what caused you to not have the desire to spend time with Him. Tell God you know you've been distant. That you know something has gotten in between you. Name what that something is. Let God know that you desire to find your way back to Him but you just don't know how to. Be honest with God. Let Him know that you need His help in rekindling your relationship with Him and you can't do it by yourself. It all starts with just talking to Him. You don't have to have a long, dragged out prayer. Just have a conversation with the One who has never stopped loving you. Just like in a natural relationship, you would just pick up the phone or meet up with that person and start talking to them. Do the same with your Creator. Don't think of how. Don't think of when. Just do it! Just open your mouth and start talking.

Instead, let us test and examine our ways.
Let us turn back to the Lord.
Lamentations 3:40
New Living Translation (NLT)

Have you identified what that "something" is that came between you and God?

Did you have a conversation with God and just let it all out? How are you feeling after that conversation?

Did you get quiet to hear what God has to say to you? If not, do it now.

Prayer:

God, I am the one who let "something" come between us and I am the one admitting I need You to help me get over that "something." I can't do it without You God. I've tried and the only thing that has happened is that I've allowed distance to come between us. I don't want to be distant from You, God. I want to be near You.

I want to be in Your presence. I want to feel Your presence around me. I want You, God. I want the relationship we once had. I want to hear Your voice again. I want to feel wrapped in Your love again. Take me back in Your arms God. I long for You. I want You. I need You. I love You. I desire You. I'm sorry I distanced myself. I'm sorry I've allowed things (name them) come between us. I don't ever want that to happen again so I'm going to need You to help me make sure this doesn't happen again. Strengthen me, O God, that if those things come up again, I'm strong enough not to allow them to put a wedge between us. I don't have want anything to come between us again. I need You and I want You. I love You God. Thank You for loving me even when I was distant. In Jesus' name I pray, Amen.

But I called on your name, Lord,
from deep within the pit.
You heard me when I cried,
"Listen to my pleading!
Hear my cry for help!"
Yes, you came when I called;
you told me, "Do not fear."
Lamentations 3:55-57
New Living Translation (NLT)

DAY FOUR

Nearer Than You Think

The difference in our natural relationships and our relationship with God– God. In a natural relationship, when there's distance between us and the one we're in relationship with, there is really distance. That's where it's different in our relationship with God. He's never distant from us. He's nearer than we think and realize. Although we may have walked away from Him, He never leaves us.

Behold, I stand at the door and knock. If
anyone hears My voice and opens the door,
I will come in to him and dine with him,
and he with Me.
Revelation 3:20
New King James Version (NKVJ)

This Scripture pertains to those who once where in relationship with God and for whatever reason, drifted away. Do you hear what it's saying? Just come back. God wants you back! Through it all, He's stayed right there patiently waiting for you. That's how much He loves you. That's how much He adores you. That's how much He wants to be in relationship with you. Who do you think we got the yearning and desire to be in love and be in relationship from? God, of course.

Just open the door to your heart and let God back in. This is one of the beginning steps to re-establishing your relationship with Him. As you open the door, watch and see if He doesn't take you in His arms again. He's just that in love with you and just that crazy about you. He promised He would never leave us or forsake us and He's a keeper of His word.

For He Himself has said,
"I will never leave you nor forsake you."
Hebrews 13:5b
New King James Version (NKJV)

Intimacy can be defined as really knowing
another person and being known by that person.
When you're intimate with someone, you feel
close to that person. In a natural relationship,
when something occurs to damage that
relationship, you start to feel distant from one
another. I'm so glad our relationship with God is
a supernatural relationship. When something
causes us to pull away from Him, He does not
withdraw away from us but is constantly there
trying to woo us back to Him.

The Lord has appeared of old to me,
saying: "Yes, I have loved you with an
everlasting love; Therefore with
lovingkindness I have drawn you.
Jeremiah 31:3
New King James Version (NKJV)

Now that you know that God is nearer than
you feel or think, you may ask yourself how do
you draw back near to Him. Remember in the
beginning of this devotional when I spoke of
desire? It's that desire that initiates the drawing
you back to God. You desire to be back into

relationship with Him. You desire what you once had with Him. You desire to spend time with Him and hear His voice. You desire to spend time in His word. That desire is key. As you desire intimacy with God, you begin taking steps to draw yourself back into relationship with Him.

One thing I have desired of the Lord,
That I will seek:
That I may dwell in the house of the Lord
All the days of my life,
To behold the beauty of the Lord,
And to inquire in His Temple.
Psalm 27:4
New King James Version (NKJV)

Now that you know God never left you and has always been there, you don't have to believe the lie that the devil told you – that God is mad at you and left you. God promised He would never leave us or forsake us and despite the distance that appeared between you when you stopped praying to Him, talking to Him, spending time with Him, and reading His word, He still remained right there in love with you.

Do you get it now? No matter how distant you grew to God, He yet remained right there for you. That's how deep His love is for you. You don't have to believe the devil's lies – that God doesn't forgive you, that God is upset with you, that God doesn't hear you. All lies because nothing can separate you from His love for you.

> *And I am convinced that nothing can*
> *ever separate us from God's love.*
> *Neither death nor life, neither angels*
> *nor demons, neither our fears for*
> *today nor our worries about tomorrow—*
> *not even the powers of hell can separate*
> *us from God's love.*
> *No power in the sky above or in the earth*
> *below—indeed, nothing in all creation will*
> *ever be able to separate us from the love*
> *of God that is revealed in Christ Jesus*
> *our Lord.*
> *Romans 8:38-39*
> *New Living Translation (NLT)*

Did you think God was mad at you? Why?

Because the relationship had fizzled, did you feel like God was no where to be found? What contributed to that?

What lies did the devil try to tell you?

What answers do you find in the Word (Bible) concerning these lies? Write them down and rehearse them so when the enemy comes at you with these lies again, you can answer him with the Word of God just like Jesus did in the wilderness.

How do you feel knowing God never left you or forsaked you? That He was always nearer than you felt like He was.

Prayer,

Father God, I felt so distant from You. At times I couldn't feel You near me and thought You'd left me. Now I realize that You were always there. Just as it says in Your Word, You will never leave me or forsake me and there's nothing that can separate me from Your love.

Thank You God for loving me so. Thank You for remaining steadfast in our relationship even when I waivered and distanced myself away from You. I'm grateful for Your love, Your mercy, and Your grace that You pour out upon me each day. Forgive me for ever doubting You God. Forgive me for ever doubting Your love for me. Forgive me for ever doubting You were not mindful of me. According to Your Word, you are always mindful of me. I'm so glad to be back in Your arms again God. You were always right there with Your arms outstretched to me. I just had to run back into them. Thank You for giving me the chance to run back to You. In Jesus' name I pray. Amen.

DAY FIVE

God, I'm Sorry

Relationships tend to start out great, then something happens and that wonderfulness disappears. We tend to think that maybe that relationship wasn't worth it. But when you know that's the "one," you make up your mind to do whatever it takes to get back into relationship with that person. You know God is the "One" so are you ready to do what it takes to get back into relationship with Him. Just like with your natural "Boo," you start to mend the relationship by saying "I'm sorry." The same is true with God. Let Him know you're sorry. Repent for separating yourself from Him and running away from Him when you should have been running toward Him.

Now I rejoice, not that you were made

*sorry, but that your sorrow lead to
repentance.*
2 Corinthians 7:9a
New King James Version (NKJV)

Being sorrowful for your actions can result in changed behavior. Your actually being sorry for allowing things or situations to put a wedge in your relationship with God can also help prevent it from happening again. That's why repentance is so important. In addition to apologizing to God, you also need to repent.

What is repentance? What does it mean to repent? Many people understand the term "repent" to mean to turn away from sin. Like turning away from it and walking away from it. When you repent, you do more than just being sorrowful and saying you're sorry. You make up your mind that you're not going to sin anymore and turn your back on it or walk away from it.

*For the kind of sorrow God wants us to
experience leads us away from sin and
results in salvation. There's no regret for*

*that kind of sorrow. But worldly sorrow,
which lacks repentance, results in spiritual
death.*
2 Corinthians 7:10
New Living Translation (NLT)

So, when you go to God apologizing for how you allowed your intimacy with Him fizzle out, make up your mind that whatever lead to you distancing yourself, you will not allow to separate you from God again. Acknowledge your role in the separation and whatever that something, someone, issue, or situation was that caused the wedge between you and God. Make up your mind that you will not allow it to put distance between you and your Creator again. If it caused you to sin against God in addition to separating yourself from God, repent and press in even closer to God.

How is apologizing and repenting different?

What caused the wedge in your intimate relationship with God?

Did it cause you to sin? How?

When you apologized and repented to God, how did it make you feel?

What can you do to prevent that something, someone, issue, or situation from driving a wedge in your relationship with God in the future?

Prayer:

God, please forgive me for _____ *(say what it is – being mad at God, screaming at God, cursing at God, not wanting to talk to God, not wanting to listen to God – whatever it was). I repent of this right now in the name of Jesus. I was wrong to let* _____ *(say what the situation or issue was) get in between us. I should have never allowed that thing to separate me from You. Strengthen me to be like You and not allow anything to separate me from You again.*

God, I confess the following sins _____ *that I committed and ask for Your forgiveness. I repent of these sins in the name of Jesus. I desire to walk holy and upright in Your sight. I need Your Holy Spirit to be my Teacher and my Guide to show me how to walk holy and upright in Your sight. I acknowledge I can't do it on my own and need Your help. Reveal to me if there is any unconfessed sin in my life so I may renounce it and repent of it. My desire is to be pleasing to You and in relationship with You. I never want anything to come between us again. In Jesus' name I pray. Amen.*

DAY SIX

What Is Intimacy with God?

Intimacy is a state of being intimate. It's marked by a friendship developing through a long association. You connect deeply with that person. That's how our relationship with God should be. To get to that intimacy with God, it must develop through a long association. In other words, it develops through spending time with Him. When we neglect spending time with Him, that intimacy dwindles.

O God, you are my God;
I earnestly search for you.
My soul thirsts for you;
my whole body longs for you
in this parched and weary land
where there is no water.
Psalm 63:1

New Living Translation (NLT)

If you're reading this book, chances are you realize you've lost that intimacy with God and you acknowledge you haven't been spending time with Him like you should, to develop that intimacy. Intimacy with God is crucial. We were created to be intimate with God – in close relationship with our Creator. When Jesus died on the cross for our sins, the veil was torn so we could go to God directly. Prior to that, the people of God had to have a priest to go to God on their behalf. When Jesus died on the cross, He changed that. His sacrifice meant we could go directly to the Father to talk to Him ourselves.

Then Jesus shouted out again, and he released his spirit. At that moment the curtain in the sanctuary of the Temple was torn in two, top to bottom. The earth shook, rocks split apart,
Matthew 27:50-51
New Living Translation (NLT)

The temple consisted of the Outer Court, the

Inner Court, the Holy Place, and the Most Holy Place. The priests could only enter the Holy Place. The priests could only enter the Most Holy Place once a year to atone for the sins of the people. There was a curtain separating the Holy Place from the Most Holy Place. At Christ's death, that curtain was torn in two, which symbolized the barrier between God and humanity was removed. Now the people could freely approach God through Christ's death on the cross. Because you can freely approach God, you can have an intimate relationship with Him.

I lie awake thinking of you,
meditating on you through the night.
Psalm 63:6
New Living Translation (NLT)

In a natural relationship, when you're deeply and madly in love with a person, you yearn for them. You want to look into their eyes. You want to hear their voice. Your heart beats rapidly at the thought of them. Just the mention of their name makes you smile. You just want to be in their presence. You just want to be near them. You just want them. That's how we should be in our relationship with God. When we have an intimate relationship with Him, our hearts pant at the very thought of Him. Even as I type these words to you, my heart is panting for my Creator. Just the mere thought of a relationship with Him is taking my breath away as I ponder on the love between us. Oh, how He loves me! Oh, how He loves you! That's intimacy.

> *As the deer pants for the water brooks,*
> *So pants my soul for You, O God.*
> *My soul thirsts for God, for the living*
> *God. When shall I come and appear*
> *before God?*
> *Psalm 42:1-2*
> *New King James Version (NKJV)*

Intimacy with God brings a satisfaction beyond words. Remember a time when you were in love with someone. That person was constantly on your mind. You could have been having a bad day and just the thought of them brought a smile to your face. Someone could have just made you mad then a thought of them flashes in your mind and you forgot all about that person who made you mad as you focus on the one you love, who loves you. Their presence alone, changes your mood. It could have been the roughest day of your life, but when you're with the one you love, it seems to just fade away. That's the kind of satisfaction an intimate relationship with God has. He does all those things at a higher power or higher dosage.

Imagine having a bad day and taking it to God, and having the Creator of all begin to whisper to you that "He got you and it's going to be all right." Imagine His presence engulfing you and feeling the love He has for you. The thoughts of that bad day just fade away as He ministers to you and reminds you that He has you in the palm of His hand. I don't know about you but if sweet nothings from a person can make your toes curl, surely sweet somethings from God can cause your spirit to turn flips. He's just that awesome!

The Lord your God in your midst, The Mighty One will save; He will rejoice over you with gladness, He will quiet you with

His love, He will rejoice over you
with singing.
Zephaniah 3:17
New King James Version (NKJV)

Intimacy with another person means they know the good, the bad, and the ugly about you and vice versa. The same is true when it comes to intimacy with God. He knows the good, the bad, the ugly, and even the uglier about you yet He still loves you and wants to spend time with you. He wants to have you talk to Him through prayer and He wants to talk right back to you. He wants to reveal revelation to you when you're reading His word. He wants to be close to you despite the good, bad, and ugly about you. He knows your flaws but loved you so much that He sacrificed His only begotten son to provide a way back to him despite the flaws and sin.

For God so loved the world that He
gave His only begotten Son, that whoever
believes in Him should not perish but
have everlasting life. For God did not send
His Son into the world to condemn the

world, but that the world through
Him might be saved.
John 3:16-17
New King James Version (NKJV)

If you could give a definition of what it means to have an intimate relationship which God, what would it say?

How can you improve your intimacy with God?

What steps are you planning to take to improve your intimacy with God?

Prayer:

God, show me new ways to love You and adore You. I desire to grow more intimate in my relationship with You. I know where I left off before I grew distant with You, but show me how to go even beyond that. I want to love in ways that words just can't describe. Forgive me for not panting after You these _____ (days, weeks, months, years). As I rekindle the flame between us, I want to love You deeply with all of

me. Thank You for never stopping Your panting after me and never giving up on me. In Jesus' name I pray. Amen.

DAY SEVEN

More Intimacy with God

Intimacy with God includes getting to know Him – who He is, His desires, His ways, His Word, what pleases Him, what displeases Him, what's on His mind, His promises, how He does things, why He does things, why He doesn't do somethings, etc. It's the opportunity for you to get to know your Creator. It's important for you to really know God and not just know about God. You get to know God through an intimate relationship with Him. After all, there's a difference between knowing about someone and knowing someone. Knowing about someone means there's no relationship between you and you're admiring them or being mindful of them from afar off. Knowing someone means you're in relationship with them and know things about them through the close association and relationship you share. It's through an intimate relationship with God that you will really begin to know Him.

Show me Your ways, O Lord;
Teach me Your paths,
Lead me in your Truth and teach me,
For You are the God of my salvation;
On You I wait all the day.
Psalm 25:4-5
New King James Version (NKJV)

How do you get to know God? Go back to a time when you were in love with someone. It's the same way you got to know that person. Did you not spend vast amounts of time together? You hung out together. You talked on the phone through the wee hours of the night. You may have texted each other endlessly. You left messages for one another. You just had to always be around that person and in contact with them. You asked each other questions like, "What's your favorite color," "What's your favorite food(s)," "What's your favorite song," et cetera. The two of you wanted to really know each other.

That's how an intimate relationship with God should be. You should desire to spend vast amounts of time with Him and get to really know Him. In that intimate time together, He will teach you what He likes and don't like. He'll provide you with guidance and advice. He'll show you His promises in His Word. He'll teach you His ways and may even share some secrets with you. The closer you are to Him, the closer He is to you. You may even become a friend of God. There were only a few in the Bible who God called His friend. Who knows, you could be the next one.

> *And so it happened just as the Scriptures say: "Abraham believed God, and God counted him as righteous because of his faith." He was even called the friend of God.*
> *James 2:23*
> *New Living Translation (NLT)*

To create a close and intimate relationship with God, you have to put forth the time and effort. You have to make time for God. Don't get caught up on the time – whether early or first thing in the morning or later in the day – just make time for Him. God understands your schedule. Decide on a time you can give to Him each day and know that the time may change from day to day. God isn't caught up on it just has to be the same time each day, He just wants you to spend time with Him each day no matter what time of day it is. Also, don't get caught up on the place. Some may spend time with Him while driving in the car. Some may spend time with Him at home. Some may go on a walk and spend time with Him. Just make time during your day for Him. Strive to make time to just talk to Him. Strive to make time to pray to Him. Strive to make time to read your Bible or listen to your audio Bible. Strive to make time to actually study your Bible and dive into Scripture.

Just take it day by day. The mistake we often make when we've distanced ourselves from God is trying to jump in where we left off. Create something new in your rekindling of the relationship with God. Don't beat yourself up or try to pick up where you left off. Start afresh again. Some of you may remember an old song called "Take Me Back." In a verse of the song it's asking God to take you back to where you first believed. Start afresh. Start over again from the beginning with God. He understands. We often fail when we try to pick up where we left off. Just the stress of it is enough to make you give up. Don't do that. Don't put that stress on yourself. Just start again. Go back to where you first believed and received Him.

Don't try to pick up where you left off. I'm going to stress this point because so many do it and give up from the stress of not being able to just jump in where they left off in their relationship with God. God is always doing something new and He just may want to do something new in His relationship with you. Don't get stuck on how you used to spend time with Him or when you used to spend time with Him. Don't get stuck on how you used to pray, how you used to worship, how you used to fast, how you used to read and study the Bible. Talk to God and ask Him, "God, how should I do these things now. How should I approach our rekindled relationship now?"

*"But forget all that – it is nothing compared
to what I am going to do. For I am about
to do something new. See, I have already
begun! Do you not see it?*
Psalm 43:18-19a
New Living Translation (NLT)

Communication is also important in your intimate relationship with God. Some of us can learn the mistakes of how we communicated in our past relationships with people. Did you talk too much and not allow the other person to get a word in? Did you not listen and really hear what the other person had to say? Don't do this in your relationship with God.

*A wise man will hear and increase
learning, And a man of understanding
will attain wise counsel,*
Proverbs 1:5
New King James Version (NKJV)

To grow in intimacy with Him, you must know how to communicate with Him. There are times when you're going to need to talk to Him, but there are also times when you're going to just have to be quiet and listen to Him while He's doing all the talking. The communication with God has to be two-way communication. There are times when you should talk and there are times when you should listen while He talks.

In your intimate relationship with God, there should be a dialogue between the two of you. God is a gentleman and won't dominate the conversation, and neither should you. Value that He has things He wants to say to you. It may be audibly, or it may be through His Word, the Bible. But know, He always has something He wants to say to you so you will have to learn to be quiet and listen no matter how long it takes.

And the Lord came and called as before,
"Samuel! Samuel!"
And Samuel replied,
"Speak, your servant is listening."
1 Samuel 3:10
New Living Translation (NLT)

Communicate with God as you read the Bible

– His Word. As you study and read His Word, ask Him to reveal the revelation of the Scripture(s) to you. "God, what are you saying to me through this Scripture? God, what do you want me to know through this Scripture? God, how do I apply this Scripture to my life or situation? God, what's the meaning of this Scripture?" Then learn to get quiet and expect to hear the answers to your questions from God. Don't just ask the questions and jump up and go about your day. Just take the time to get quiet and wait on His answers.

But those who wait on the Lord
Shall renew their strength;
They shall mount up with wings like eagles,
They shall run and not be weary,
They shall walk and not faint.
Isaiah 40:31
New King James Version (NKJV)

Something to be careful about in your intimate relationship with God is quantity versus quality. This has been the downfall of many relationships with God. Don't get caught up on the quantity, meaning the time. Focus of the quality of your intimate relationship with God and not the quantity. It's about spending time with Him not the amount of time you spend with Him. It's about praying to Him and not getting caught up on the amount of time you pray. It's about fasting when needed even if you have to take baby steps. It's not about how long you fast. Make whatever time you spend with Him count and don't worry about the clock. God isn't focused on the clock (time). He's focused on just being with you and having you just come to be with Him. Whatever time you spend with God, make it quality time. Make the most out of it.

And He said to them, "Come aside by
yourselves to a deserted place and rest a while.
Mark 6:31a
New King James Version (NKJV)

Then Jesus said, "Let's go off by ourselves to
a quiet place and rest awhile."
Mark 6:31a
New Living Translation (NLT)

Another thing to remember when it comes to your intimacy with God is not to make your intimate relationship with Him so goal focused. "God, I need a new car. I need a new job. I want to be married. I need more money. I want a child." Learn to get into the habit of spending time with God just because you love Him and adore Him. Just because you just want to be in His presence without asking Him for anything. You just want Him to wrap His arms around you. In your natural relationship, you wouldn't just spend time with that person to get something out of them. You often did it just because you simply wanted to be with them. Do the same with God. He is the ultimate love of your life. Spend close and intimate time with Him just because you want to be with Him. You just want to be in His presence. There's a saying that says we should seek God's face and not His hands.

When You said, "Seek My face,"
My heart said to You,
"Your face, Lord, I will seek."
Psalm 27:8
New King James Version (NKJV)

My heart has heard you say,
"Come and talk with me."
And my heart responds,
"Lord, I am coming."
Psalm 27:8
New Living Translation (NLT)

Throughout the Bible, you see many people who had close and intimate relationships with God despite their shortcomings and mistakes. Just look at Abraham – who lied, who God called His friend. Look at Moses – who smote the rock and didn't speak eloquently, who God chose to lead the people of God out of Egypt. Look at David – who committed adultery then had the husband killed, who God said was a man after His own heart. Look at the Paul who used to be called Saul – who killed Christians, but God used to help spread the Gospel.

Despite how your previous relationship with God ended, He's waiting to start a new one with you. Despite your good, your bad, and your ugly, God is still in love with you and wants to have an intimate relationship with you.

I can never escape your Spirit! I can
never get away from your presence!
Psalm 139:7
New Living Translation (NLT)

**Think of ways to spend time with God.
What excuses prevented you from spending
time with God before? How can you avoid
those excuses?**

**What's something new you can do in your
intimate relationship with God?**

**How as your communication with God prior to
your relationship becoming distant? What did
you learn from that?**

Prayer:

*Father God, thank you for the opportunity to
have a close and intimate relationship with You.
I thank You that You don't hold my past against
me and welcome me back into Your presence.
Forgive me if I haven't communicated with You
as I should in the past. I want to come into Your*

presence to talk with You and sit quiet before You. Forgive me if I took our relationship for granted before. I never want to take You or our relationship for granted. Lord I strive to seek Your face and not your hand. I just want You God. In Jesus' name I pray, Amen.

DAY EIGHT

The Unpleasant Conversation

In any relationship that was fizzled out, there has always been a reason. When you reconnect with that person, in the beginning of the reconnection, you may not talk about what led to the relationship ending or slowing down. You only want to enjoy the reconnection and getting to know each other again. So, you don't bring it up or mention it. Deep down, you know the two of you have to eventually have that unpleasant conversation of what went wrong the first time. It's the moment you dreaded but it's the moment you know has to come. It's the same in our relationship with God.

Something happened that led to you getting more and more distant from God. You can't ignore any longer. It may hurt to talk about it, but it's time for you and God to have that conversation. If your relationship is going to last this time, you have to talk to Him about why you distanced yourself that last time around. Just be honest with Him. It's time to get it all out.

> *Casting all your care upon Him,*
> *for He cares for you.*
> *1 Peter 5:7*
> *New King James Version (NKJV)*

Now that you've moved toward God to rekindle your intimate relationship with Him, now it's time to discuss the unpleasant moment or moments that lead to the wedge in your relationship.

"God, I'm mad or upset at You because…" What's your because? What's the unpleasant experience, situation, or issue that led to you being mad at God? What hurt you to the point you chose to walk away from Him or distance yourself from Him? What was so painful or hurtful that you only could see the solution to distance yourself from God? Take it to God.

Come to Me, all you who labor and are
heavy laden, and I will give you rest.
Matthew 11:28
New King James Version (NKJV)

"God, I'm upset because You didn't keep Your Word. You promised me a child and me and my spouse have been waiting 10 years. You promised me a spouse and I've kept myself pure for the last 18 years and I'm still single. You promised me a promotion at work and they gave it to someone   else. You promised me a job and I've been on numerous interviews but no one has hired me. God, I feel like You lied to me. You promised me some things and I haven't received them yet and I'm mad about it."

And "don't sin by letting anger control you."
Don't let the sun go down while you are still angry.
Ephesians 4:26
New Living Translation (NLT)

Don't sin by letting anger control you.
Think about it overnight and remain silent.

Psalm 4:4
New Living Translation (NLT)

It's ok to let God know you're upset about the situation or issue. The devil may have told you that you're going to hell for being upset with God or even tried to flip the script on you and tell you that God is mad at you. All lies!

God already knew you were upset. Now have a conversation with Him about what you are upset disappointed about. Do you feel angry because you haven't received His promises yet? Guess what, God can't lie so if He said it, you can trust He meant it and it will manifest.

"God is not a man, that He should lie,
Nor a son of man, that He should repent.
Has He said, and will He not do?
Or has He spoken, and will He not make it good?
Numbers 23:19
New King James Version (NKJV)

If God promised you something, it will come to pass. Just hold on a little longer. Time messes us up. Because some time has passed, you may have thought that God forgot about you or changed His mind? He didn't forget about you and He definitely didn't change His mind. Maybe the timing isn't right. Maybe sin on your part delayed it. Maybe it's something He needs you to do or stop doing? Maybe someone who had a part in it didn't do their part and He has to change the route by which He brings what He promised you to pass. Now is the time to talk to God about it and find out what needs to be done. Maybe there's nothing to be done and it's simply a matter of just waiting patiently.

Wait on the Lord; Be of good courage,
And He shall strengthen your heart;
Wait, I say, on the Lord!
New King James Version (NKJV)

But if we look forward to something we don't yet
have, we must wait patiently and confidently.
Romans 8:25
New Living Translation (NLT)

"God, I'm mad or upset at You because You

let my mom or dad die. You let my child die. You gave me my spouse then You took them to be with You. You took them too soon. I didn't get to say goodbye. I didn't get to say what I wanted to say to them. We didn't have enough time together. It's not fair God! It's just not fair!" Does any of this sound familiar to some of you?

I can actually say I have an idea of how you're feeling. My husband and I experienced great loss of every child we've conceived and I too was mad at God and told Him so. I too felt He didn't keep His promise to me, and told Him so. I too remember uttering the words "It's not fair." Yes, I have an idea, but I also had to take this journey that I'm leading you on back into relationship with Him.

When we lose someone we love, it's an unimaginable hurt. We never think we'll get over it and even feel bad if years go by and we're still grieving. There's nothing wrong with you and it's ok. It's also ok to tell God how hurt you were or still are by it and that played a part in distancing yourself from Him. After multiple miscarriages I actually didn't want to talk to God, so I stopped. There were times He tried to talk to me to comfort me and I ignored Him. Yet in His mercy, He never gave up on wooing me back. And when I was finally ready to have the unpleasant conversation, He listened as I poured my heart out to Him. Then I listened as He comforted me and let me know how He hurt with me. This was the beginning to becoming "us" again. The beginning of a renewed relationship between us and the same can be for you.

If you want to scream, scream. If you want to cry, cry. Just go to God and have the unpleasant conversation with Him then allow Him to wrap His arms around You and comfort you through it. He's been waiting to do that. He waited until you were ready. And from my guess, by you purchasing and reading this devotional, you're ready too.

Let my cry come before You, O Lord;
Give me understanding according to Your word.
New King James Version (NKJV)

Are you mad or upset at God? Why?

Are you disappointed with or hurt by God? Why?

Try having the unpleasant conversation with God concerning these things. How did it make you feel?

What promises are you still waiting on from God? Talk to Him about them and ask why they haven't come yet.

Prayer:

God, I have been mad or upset with You because _____ (tell Him why). I felt like You didn't keep Your Word, but I know You're not a man that You should lie and if you said it then it will come to pass. Forgive me for being upset with You. Forgive me for ever doubting You. Help me to understand the delay or the waiting period. Help me to understand why _____ (name it) had to happen, because I don't understand. I don't want to allow these things that hurt me or come between us again. I need Your help God and I need You to comfort me through this. The pain is/was unbearable and I didn't think I would make it. Restore my joy again according to Your lovingkindness. I'm pouring my heart out to You God, now take me in Your arms and comfort me and guide me through this. I need understanding and guidance that can only come from You. Show me what I need to do or stop doing so that Your promises to me come to pass. If it's no action for me to take, hold my hand as I patiently wait upon You. In Jesus' name I pray, Amen.

**For this prayer, add the unpleasant converstation to it. Pour your heart out to God and tell Him everything on your mind.

DAY NINE
Still Mad?

Now that you've had the unpleasant conversation, you may feel better or you may still be mad or upset. You may still be wrestling with the "why" questions. Why didn't God answer your prayer? Why didn't God do this or do that? Why did God allow this or that? Why, why, why? And even though you had the conversation with God about why you distanced yourself from Him, truth be told, you're still mad.

But it displeased Jonah exceedingly, and
he became angry.
Jonah 4:1
New King James Version (NKJV)

Many people have struggled with the question of if it's ok to be mad with God. They knew they were mad at Him but were torn because they didn't know if they could be mad at God. Is it right to be mad at God? Many still struggle with that question.

Then the Lord said, "Is it right for you
to be angry?"
Jonah 4:4
New King James Version (NKJV)

That's a question you have to ask yourself. "Is it right for you to be angry with God?" In the Scripture above, this is what God asked Jonah when Jonah became angry with God. After you ask yourself that question, you next need to ask yourself why exactly are you angry. Did God do something so horrible? When you ponder that, I bet you'll find out it's not something God did but how you interpreted it.

"My thoughts are nothing like your
thoughts," says the Lord. "And my
ways are far beyond anything you
could imagine.
Isaiah 55:8

New Living Translation (NLT)

So many times, we think we know how God thinks and why He did this or didn't do that. He tells us in this verse that His thoughts are nothing like our thoughts. So, when we're thinking He's acted unfair toward us about a situation or issue, it's not that. Instead of trying to fit His actions into the box of our own understanding, we need to go to Him to get the true understanding of why He allowed or didn't allow something instead of just rushing into being mad about it. Could the truth be we're made based off our understanding of the situation or issue? Since when did our understanding trump God's?

"God, I'm mad at You because You haven't delivered on Your Word to me. You haven't given me this or that like You promised me." Earlier in this devotional, I talked about God's timing. Maybe it's not time for you to have this or that. What if you haven't prepared yourself for what God promised you? God will never give you something you're not prepared for. It just might not be the time right now. I know that can be hard to grasp in this microwave world that we live in. We want everything immediately and right now. We don't want to wait for it. We treat God this way when it comes to the blessings and promises He promised us. We tend to have the mentality that if He said it, we don't have to wait for it. He should give it to us now. So, once again, should we get mad at God for this microwave mentality we have? Is it His fault we must sometimes wait on what He promised? Certainly not. One thing is for sure, if He promised it, you will receive it. He is a keeper of His word!

It is the same with my word. I send it out,
and it always produces fruit.
It will accomplish all I want it to,
and it will prosper everywhere I send it.
Isaiah 55:11
New Living Translation (NLT)

On day 8, we learned that God is not a man that He should lie, and we see above that Scripture declares when He speaks a word it goes out and accomplishes what He said. You can rest assured that if He said it then it shall come to pass. Just be patient.

Tragedy happens in all our lives and when it does happen, we find ourselves asking God, "Why?" It's just something wired in each and every one of us to ask the question "why" when tragedy or bad things happen. We just want to know why it had to happen. "Why God, why?" We ask questions like, "Why did this have to happen to me? To him or her? To them? To us? Why God, why?" We then want to put the blame on God. "God, You didn't have to let this or that happen. You could have stopped it. Why didn't You stop it? Why didn't you give him, her, or them more time? It's not fair God." We criticize God's actions or lack of actions in the situation. We start to place blame on Him saying He could have stopped it or He could have prevented it.

"Do you still want to argue with the Almighty? You are God's critic, but do you have the answers?"
Job 40:2
New Living Translation (NLT)

After questioning God, we then tend to become angry with Him about the thing that occurred or didn't occur. We get so angry with him that we question His sovereignty and His actions. We may even raise our voice in anger toward Him, forgetting He is God.

> *"Will you discredit my justice and*
> *Condemn me just to prove you are*
> *right? Are you as strong as God?*
> *Can you thunder with a voice like*
> *his? All right, put on your glory and*
> *splendor, your honor and majesty.*
> *Give vent to your anger.*
> *Let it overflow against the proud.*
> *Job 40:8-11*
> *New Living Translation (NLT)*

You must remind yourself – even in your anger against God – that God has not lost control of anything. He hasn't allowed something to happen that should not have happened in your opinion. He didn't forget His promises to you. He is not absent minded or forgetful. He isn't merciless or unjust. God is sovereign and He has everything under control even if you understand it or not. He doesn't have to justify anything to us. Yet, in His mercy and compassion, He understands you're upset and wants to comfort you.

Have you ever seen a relationship where the woman became so irate and upset that she just started screaming and throwing stuff at the man? She may have even tried to hit him in her frustration and anger, then you see the man grab her and just hold her tight saying how much he loves her and that everything will be alright. That's what God wants to do to you. He just wants to hold you and let you know that despite that situation or issue that He loves you and everything will be alright.

So back to the original question – is it ok to be mad at God. The answer may surprise you. Did you know that a fit of anger is sin? Yep, the Bible clearly states so.

When you follow the desires of your
sinful nature, the results are very clear:

sexual immorality, impurity, lustful
pleasures, idolatry, sorcery, hostility,
*quarreling, jealousy, **outbursts of anger**,*
selfish ambition, dissension, division,
envy, drunkenness, wild parties, and other
sins like these. Let me tell you again, as
I have before, that anyone living that sort
of life will not inherit the Kingdom of God.
Galatians 5:19-21
New Living Translation (NLT)

The Word of God tells us to do away with anger.

But now is the time to get rid of anger,
rage, malicious behavior, slander, and
dirty language.
Colossians 3:8
New Living Translation (NLT)

If we hold onto anger against anyone, especially God, bitterness and resentment can set it. Once those set in, they can lead to an abundance of sin on our part. In addition to anger, the Bible also instructs us to get rid of any bitterness as well.

Get rid of all bitterness, rage, anger,
harsh words, and slander, as well as
all types of evil behavior.
Ephesians 4:31
New Living Translation (NLT)

God recognizes anger and bitterness as types of evil behavior. So, I ask again, you still mad at God? If you've been mad at God and now realize it's a sin, confess this sin to God and ask for His forgiveness. He is just to forgive you. You may not have known it was a sin when you initially became angry with Him. After reading the devotional today, you now realize it's a sin so repent and ask for God's forgiveness. Remember, when you know better, you do better. You now know better when it comes to being angry with God.

God understands when you are angry with Him. He wants you to be real with Him and let Him know how you're feeling. He does not want you to hide it. Just don't allow the anger to cause you to sin against God. Put whatever it is that's caused you to be angry with Him into His hands and trust Him.

After finding out what Scripture says about being angry, how are you feeling?

Have you repented and asked God's forgiveness for being angry with Him?

Do you think you were initially angry with God because you felt like you had no control in or over that situation or circumstance?

Now that you've had time to calm down, what is your perception of why you became so angry or disappointed over the situation or circumstance?

Now that you've calmed down, what would you like to say to God?

Prayer:

Father God, please forgive me for sinning by being angry with you. I didn't realize it before but now I know according to your Word that it's a since and I'm sincerely sorry. I also repent and apologize for not trusting You about _____ (say what the situation, issue, or circumstance is or was). Forgive me for not trusting You even when I didn't understand what You were doing. I'm sorry I ever questioned You as if You were not still in control. I thank You that even when I was angry with You, disappointed with You, upset with You, and frustrated with You – You yet understood and still loved me. I will come to You in prayer instead of getting angry or frustrated. I will learn to trust You more despite how the situation or circumstance looks. Thank You for Your mercy and grace, which is new every day. I love You God! In Jesus' name I pray, Amen.

DAY TEN
Forgiveness

Forgiveness can be defined as releasing someone from anger or resentment. When you forgive someone, you release your feelings of anger and resentment against them whether they deserve it or not. The Bible command us to forgive others who have wronged us.

But if you refuse to forgive others, your
Father will not forgive your sins.
Matthew 6:15
New Living Translation (NLT)

In relationships, things tend to happen where sometimes it feels hard to forgive the other person for. We tend to hold onto the hurt and pain, playing it over and over again in our minds, going through the spiral of emotional feelings, which allows bitterness and resentment to build. Whatever the other person did to upset the relationship, sometimes it just feels hard to forgive. Thankfully God is merciful to forgive us when we've walked away from or distanced ourselves from the relationship, we have with Him.   Surely if He is quick to forgive us, shouldn't we also be quick to forgive others.

> *and forgive us our sins, as we have forgiven*
> *those who sin against us.*
> *Matthew 6:12*
> *New Living Translation (NLT)*

> *But when you are praying, first forgive*
> *anyone you are holding a grudge against,*
> *so that your Father in heaven will forgive*
> *your sins, too."*
> *Mark 11:25*
> *New Living Translation (NLT)*

In a relationship gone bad, for there to be reconciliation, there must be forgiveness. In order for there to be reconciliation in your relationship with God, there must be forgiveness. When you want to rekindle your relationship with God, there's nothing too bad that you did to cause Him to stop loving you and not forgive you.

> *And I am convinced that nothing can*
> *ever separate us from God's love. Neither*
> *death nor life, neither angels nor demons,*
> *neither our fears for today nor our worries*
> *about tomorrow—not even the powers of*
> *hell can separate us from God's love.*
> *No power in the sky above or in the earth*
> *below—indeed, nothing in all creation will*
> *ever be able to separate us from the love*
> *of God that is revealed in Christ Jesus*
> *our Lord.*
> *Romans 8:38-39*
> *New Living Translation (NLT)*

When it comes to rekindling the flames of our relationship with God, it's not a matter of if you forgive God for anything. It's a matter of forgiving yourself for being upset with God and allowing something to make you run from Him when you should have run toward Him. Sometimes it's not the devil who condemns us the most, sometimes it's ourselves. You may have thrown a tantrum when you were upset with God. Before you walked away from Him and stopped praying to Him and reading your Bible, you may have yelled at Him and said some mean things to Him. You may have outright doubted Him and even told Him you didn't believe Him. Yep, you may have done those things and know that you want to reconnect with Him, you may be feeling ashamed, condemned, convicted, and unworthy of His love. You may be having a hard time forgiving yourself for acting a fool with God. But for the reconciliation to work, you must forgive yourself. Otherwise, you will allow the shame of your actions prevent you from drawing near to God.

> *"Assuredly, I say to you, all sins will be*
> *forgiven the sons of men, and whatever*
> *blasphemies they may utter;*
> *Mark 3:28*
> *New King James Version (NKJV)*

You may be feeling bad for your actions or even accusations toward God, but go to Him and repent and apologize. He is just to forgive you. If you go to Him and confess your since, He will forgive you.

If we confess our sins, He is faithful and just to forgive us our sins and to cleanse us from all unrighteousness.
1 John 1:9
New King James Version (NKJV)

Because of God's unconditional love for you, when you ask Him for forgiveness, He will grant it to you. He understands the pain and emotions you were feeling when you distanced yourself from Him. He's been right there beside you, waiting for you to return to Him. He's been waiting for you so run into His arms and ask for forgiveness for your actions. He's ready to rekindle your relationship.

Did you feel ashamed for being upset or angry with God? How do you feel now?

Did you feel like God wouldn't forgive you? Why?

Did you feel like what you did was too terrible for God to forgive you? Why?

Prayer:

God, forgive me for my actions toward You. Forgive me for _____ (describe your actions). I acted toward You and spoke to You in ways that I should not have, and I am ashamed of how I acted toward You. I lay my guilt, heartache, and shame down before You. I repent of my actions and ask You to please forgive me. I thank You for forgiving me, for being patient with me, and for loving me unconditionally through all of this. I receive Your forgiveness, in Jesus' name. Amen.

DAY ELEVEN

Identifying Thieves

The Bible warns us about the devil, who is also referred to as a thief. He comes to steal everything he can from us and cause a division between us and God.

The thief does not come except to steal,
and to kill, and to destroy. I have come
that they may have life, and that they
may have it more abundantly.
John 10:10
New King James Version (NKJV)

Other than the "thief," the devil, what other thieves have come to steal, kill, and destroy your relationship with God? We talked about some of them like anger, in the beginning days of this devotional. What about the others that stole us away from spending time with God like we should have? Who are those thieves and how can we stop them? What was it that kept you away from your relationship with God so long? Can you put a name on it?

> *But know this, that if the master of the*
> *house had known what hour the thief*
> *would come, he would have watched*
> *and not allowed his house to be*
> *broken into.*
> *Matthew 23:43*
> *New King James Version (NKJV)*

Could one be the thief called time? Time stealers can prevent you from spending time with God as you should, and they sneak up on you. As with money, we should also be good stewards of our time. God grants us 24 hours in a day, yet time can slip away from us and if we're not careful, it can cause us to lay aside our relationship with God. Have you found yourself getting up 2 hours early to start your day, yet you keep finding yourself 15-30 minutes late for work? So, you decide to move your morning prayer and devotional time with God to after you get home from work. Well you get home from work and you have to cook dinner or help the kids with homework, so it gets pushed to right before you go to bed. But then you get distracted by a phone call, a television show, Instagram, Twitter, or Facebook, or something else. You promise God you'll make it up to him the next day but the next day is a repeat of the previous day, then before you know it, it's been week, months, and possibly years of this vicious cycle where you've put God on the backburner and neglected your relationship with Him. There is a time for everything and that includes spending intimate time with God.

> *To everything there is a season,*
> *A time for every purpose under heaven:*
> *Ecclesiastes 3:1*
> *New King James Version (NKJV)*

Could another thief be the cares of this world? This thief works with its buddy called time. See the cares of this world could rob you of time, especially spending time in relationship to God.

The Bible warns us about the cares of this world. It warns us that the cares of this world can come in and choke the word and it becomes unfruitful. The cares of this world can also choke our time and relationship with God.

> *and the cares of this world, the*
> *deceitfulness of riches, and the desires*
> *for other things entering in choke the*
> *word, and it becomes unfruitful*
> *Mark 4:19*
> *New King James Version (NKJV)*

What are the cares of this world? Some could seem so innocent that you wouldn't label them as the cares of this world. The cares of this world can include your job – breaking the glass ceiling, moving up the ladder, striving for that promotion, wanting to make partner – you could dedicate so much time to these things concerning your job that you forget to spend needed and valuable time with the One who blessed you with the job. After a while, you're rushing to get to work, excel at work, etc., that you're too busy or too tired to spend intimate time with God. Before you know it, you don't even realize that you talk to your coworkers and boos more than you talk to God. You've put him on the back burner and put your job as the front runner. Does any of this sound familiar?

> *"But that is the time to be careful!*
> *Beware that in your plenty you do*
> *not forget the Lord your God and*
> *disobey his commands, regulations,*
> *and decrees that I am giving you today.*
> *Deuteronomy 8:11*
> *New Living Translation (NLT)*

In making that money and spending less time with God, you can forget about Him to the point that you don't even miss that intimate time anymore as your focus has become your job. Don't' allow your job to take the place of God. He doesn't like anything coming before Him. That includes the job He blessed you to have.

> *"You must not have any other god but me.*
> *Exodus 20:3*
> *New Living Translation (NLT)*

For I, the Lord your God,
am a jealous God who will not tolerate
your affection for any other gods.
Exodus 20:5a
New Living Translation (NLT)

In the book of Matthew in chapter 13, we find the parable about the farmer scattering seed. The parable talks about thorny ground. Guess what? That thorny ground represents the cares of this world better known as life – your job, education, family, etc. – the distractions of life that can keep you so preoccupied and busy you don't have time to spend with God in the pursuit of these things. When God blessed you with these things, He never intended for them to take His place. If we're not careful, these things choke our relationship with God until months or even years down the road we realize we don't know the last time we spent intimate time with God. Don't allow the cares of this world to replace God. Don't allow them to choke out your valuable and intimate relationship with God.

What has taken up your time to the point you

pushed your relationship with God on the back burner?

What are some cares of this world that you've recognized in your own life that caused you to spend less and less time with God?

When did you first notice you were distancing yourself away from God? Identify what was preoccupying your time.

Prayer:

God, forgive me for allowing _____
to dominate my time to the point I placed our relationship on the back burner. I am truly sorry for that. Help me to be a better steward of the time You have blessed me with so that I won't allow _____ *to dominate my time again. I don't want to place anything or anyone above You. I want to put You first in my life so I'm asking You to give me the wisdom and understanding to know how to balance life and my relationship with You. I know I should place You first, but I admit that I get distracted by the*

cares of this world. Help me to not be distracted and to keep You first and foremost in my life. In Jesus' name I pray, Amen.

DAY TWELVE

Let's Talk

When you rekindle a natural relationship with someone, you eventually start talking to one another again. When you rekindle your spiritual and intimate relationship with God, you start talking to Him again. There will be times where you casually talk to God and there will be more so times when you will communicate with Him through prayer.

> *Hear me when I call, O God of my*
> *righteousness! You have relieved*
> *me in my distress; Have mercy on*
> *me, and hear my prayer.*
> *Psalm 4:1*
> *New King James Version (NKJV)*

Prayer is defined as communication with

God. This communication must be two sided. It can't just be one-way communication on your part. When it comes to communicating with God, there are various ways to pray. We know we can go to God in prayer and that He answers prayers, but one question that comes up is how to pray. How do you go to the Creator of all in prayer? Let's talk prayer.

> *Now it came to pass, as He was praying*
> *in a certain place, when He ceased,*
> *that one of His disciples said to Him,*
> *"Lord, teach us to pray, as John also*
> *taught his disciples."*
> *Luke 11:1*
> *New King James Version (NKJV)*

When you want to go to God in prayer, it's very important that you find a quiet place to pray. You don't want to have a lot of noise and distractions around you. You want a place where the presence of God can come in and you can hear His voice. After all, prayer is two-way communication. You will speak, but God will also speak back to you. You want a quiet and peaceful place to pray. In the Bible, in the book of Mark, we find Jesus going to a peaceful place to pray. So peaceful in fact, the disciples who were with Him kept falling asleep.

Then they came to a place which was named Gethsemane; and He said to His disciples, "Sit here while I pray." Mark 14:32 (NKJV)

Before daybreak the next morning, Jesus got up and went out to an isolated place to pray. Mark 1:35 New Living Translation (NLT)

The time is also as important as the place. Make sure you set time aside to communicate with God. You don't want to just give Him a rushed and hurried prayer where you don't even have the time to pause to hear His voice in response to you. Make sure you set aside a time when you won't be distracted and can give time and attention to God. And please don't put pressure or condemnation on yourself if it's at

different times on different days. Because of life
and the distractions it carries, you may have to
change up your time and place of prayer
occasionally. Guess what? That's ok. There will
also be times when you spontaneously pray, so the
time and location may change. Once again, that's
ok.

Read and study your Bible, and use the
Scriptures to pray to God when you can. Remind
God of His Word. If it's a certain situation or
circumstance you're going through, find the
Scriptures in the Bible that pertain to it and turn
them into a prayer to pray to God. When you just
don't know how to pray for a particular situation,
look it up in the Word of God and pray the
Scriptures back to God.

Your word is a lamp to my feet and a
light to my path.
Psalm 119:105
New King James Version (NKJV)

It's also important to pray in tongues to God.
If you have been baptized with the gift of the Holy

Spirit, one evidence of this is the gift of tongues. Speaking in tongues is a revelation gift the comes from the Holy Spirit. Speaking in tongues is speaking in a spiritual language that's unknown to man, unless someone has the gift of interpretation of tongues to reveal what's being said.

On the day of Pentecost all the believers
were meeting together in one place.
Suddenly, there was a sound from heaven
like the roaring of a mighty windstorm,
and it filled the house where they were
sitting. Then, what looked like flames of
tongues of fire appeared and settled
on each of them. And everyone present
was filled with the Holy Spirit and
began speaking in other languages,
as the Holy Spirit gave them this ability.
Acts 2:1-4
New Living Translation (NLT)

Use your tongues in prayer, especially if you're strategically praying. When you pray to God in tongues, the devil or his messengers don't know what you're saying. Also, when you just don't have the words to pray, pray in tongues. Believe it or not, there is a benefit to praying in tongues.

> *For if you have the ability to speak in*
> *tongues, you will be talking only to*
> *God, since people won't be able to*
> *understand you. You will be speaking*
> *by the power of the Spirit, but it*
> *will all be mysterious.*
> *1 Corinthians 14:2*
> *New Living Translation (NLT)*

> *And the Holy Spirit helps us in our weakness.*
> *For example, we don't know what God*
> *wants us to pray for. But the Holy Spirit*
> *prays for us with groanings that cannot*
> *be expressed in words.*
> *Romans 8:26*
> *New Living Translation (NLT)*

If you've received the baptism of the Holy Spirit, you have the Holy Spirit living on the inside of you. Practice allowing Him through praying in tongues, to intercede on your behalf. He knows exactly what to say to God when you just don't know what to pray. Trust the Holy Spirit and pray in tongues to God. Praying in tongues will also edify and strengthen you.

> *A person who speaks in tongues is*
> *strengthened personally, but one*
> *who speaks a word of prophecy*
> *strengthens the entire church.*
> *1 Corinthians 14:4*
> *New Living Translation (NLT)*

How often do you pray?

How often do you desire to pray?

Set a goal to pray every day to God.

Set a goal to do spontaneous prayer to God throughout your day.

Have you found a prayer closet – a quiet place to pray to God?

Dedicate some time each day in your prayer closet to pray and communicate with God.

Have you received the baptism of the Holy Spirit? How do you know?

Have you ever spoke or prayed in tongues? How often do or did you do it?

When is the last time you spoke or prayed in tongues?

Prayer:

Father God, my prayer is the You draw me closer to You in a more intimate relationship. Forgive me of my sins, cleanse me, and purge me. Show me Your face O God and help me to know You and Your ways. Teach me how to pray according to Your will and Your Word. I invite the Holy Spirit in to intercede for me when I just don't have the words to pray. Order my steps as I strive to make prayer and communication with You a daily activity in my life, as I realize this will strengthen our intimate relationship that I'm rekindling with You. In Jesus' name I pray, Amen.

**NOTE: *If you have not received the baptism of the Holy Spirit, pray and ask God to baptize you with the Holy Spirit with the evidence of speaking in tongues.*

DAY THIRTEEN

Love Remains

By now, you've taken the step to rekindle the flame in your relationship with God. Now, love remains. Most believe love is a feeling. The pounding of the heart or curling of the toes. Love is so much more than a feeling. What is love according to the Bible?

> *Love is patient and kind. Love is not*
> *jealous or boastful or proud or*
> *rude. It does not demand its own way.*
> *It is not irritable, and keeps no record of*
> *being wronged. It does not rejoice about*
> *injustice but rejoices whenever the truth*
> *wins out. Love never gives up, never*
> *loses faith, is always hopeful, and*
> *endures through every circumstance.*
> *1 Corinthians 13:4-7*

New Living Translation (NLT)

GOD IS LOVE!!! You can rest in that assurance. When you first established a relationship with God – when you stopped spending time with Him – through your return to Him, His love for you remained. He never stopped loving you. When you look at 1 Corinthians 13:4-7 at the Biblical definition of love, you see it describes God and how He feels about us.

God is patient and kind. Afterall, He was patient with you through your absence and return to the intimate relationship you two share. He waited patiently for you. He didn't try to force you or rush you to return. He stood right by you and patiently awaited your return to Him.

The only time God is jealous is when you put something above Him. He doesn't hide this fact as He's expressed in His Word that He's a jealous God if you put anything before Him. He not boastful, proud, or rude. He's been nothing but a gentleman with us even when we turn away from

Him. He could have demanded His own way and tried to force you to stay in the relationship. But He left you to your free will and just patiently awaited your return while never letting you know that He loved you.

You should rejoice that He's not irritable. Imagine how a person would react to you if you treated him or her like you treat God at times. A person can only handle so much rejection, yet God yet still loves you and tries to woo you back even when you've stopped wooing Him.

Remember in the early days of the devotional when I talked about repentance? Once you ask God for forgiveness and repent, He keeps no record of the wrong. He forgives you and allows you to start from a clean slate. But I warn you, please don't take that for granted.

God never gave up on you. He didn't lose faith that you wouldn't return back to Him. He knew you just needed some time. He knew you were going through some things and dealing with some strong emotions. Through it all, He didn't lose faith and was always hopeful you would run back into His loving arms. Now, that's love! A God kind of love.

If only we could love God the same way He loves us. If we did, then maybe those situations and circumstance that come with life, that we don't fully understand the reasoning behind them, couldn't drive a wedge in our relationship with God. Maybe then we wouldn't be so quick to get angry with Him. Maybe then we would realize that despite the time that has passed, God has not forgotten about us. Maybe we'd really realize that He is a keeper of His word and if He said or promised a thing, that it shall come to pass. Oh, how we should strive to better love God. How does the Bible say we should love God?

And you must love the Lord your God
with all your heart, all your soul, and
all your strength.
Deuteronomy 6:5
New Living Translation (NLT)

When you're in a human relationship and

you're in love with that person, you pour your whole heart out to him or her. Everything you are and everything you have; you are willing to give to that person because you love them so. Hoping that they will reciprocate it. If you can just pour all of yourself out to God like that. At least with God, you know He will reciprocate that and more back to you. At least you know that His love is eternal and never ending.

> *Love the Lord your God, walk in*
> *all his ways, obey his commands,*
> *hold firmly to him,*
> *and serve him with all your*
> *heart and all your soul.*
> *Joshua 22:5b*
> *New Living Translation (NLT)*

> *So be very careful to love the Lord your God.*
> *Joshua 23:11*
> *New Living Translation (NLT)*

The way to show God how much you love Him is by keeping His commands, obeying His Word, and following His ways. In this rekindled relationship with God, love Him strongly and passionately, with your whole heart and all your soul. Doesn't He deserve it? I think He loves. If you could really comprehend how deeply God loves you.

And may you have the power to
understand, as all God's people should,
how wide, how long, how high, and
how deep his love is.
Ephesians 3:18
New Living Translation (NLT)

Did you know that there's 4 types of Biblical love? They are agape, phileo, eros, and storge. These are the Greek words for love, three of which appear in the Bible. Agape is unconditional love. This is the type of love that God has for us. The Greek word "agapeo" describes the love of God. It describes God's nature as God is love.

Dear friends, let us continue to love
one another, for love comes from God.
Anyone who loves is a child of God
and knows God. But anyone who does not

*love does not know God, for God is
love. God showed how much he loved
us by sending his one and only Son into
the world so that we might have eternal
life through him. This is real love—not
that we loved God, but that he loved us and
sent his Son as a sacrifice to take away
our sins. Dear friends, since God loved
us that much, we surely ought to love
each other. No one has ever seen God.
But if we love each other, God lives in us,
and his love is brought to full expression in
us. And God has given us his Spirit as proof
that we live in him and he in us. Furthermore,
we have seen with our own eyes and now
testify that the Father sent his Son to be the
Savior of the world. All who declare that
Jesus is the Son of God have God living
in them, and they live in God. We know
how much God loves us, and we have put
our trust in his love God is love, and all who
live in love live in God, and God lives in them.
1 John 4:7-16
New Living Translation (NLT)*

Here we see that love is not a feeling but an action. God loved us so that He gave His only begotten Son – Jesus Christ – as payment to redeem us from sin. Jesus, in turn, willingly laid down His life on the cross. He didn't have to do it, but He did. That's love!

"For this is how God loved the world: He
gave his one and only Son, so that
everyone who believes in him will not
perish but have eternal life.
John 3:16
New Living Translation (NLT)

Phileo is the love that's shared between friends. Think of the love you have for your best friend. The Greek word "phileo" means you have a special interest in someone who you have a close association or friendship with. We see an example of this type of love between David and Jonathan in the Bible.

After David had finished talking with Saul,
he met Jonathan, the king's son. There
was an immediate bond between them,

for Jonathan loved David.
1 Samuel 18:1
New Living Translation (NLT)

And Jonathan made David reaffirm his
vow of friendship again, for Jonathan
loved David as he loved himself.
1 Samuel 20:17
New Living Translation (NLT)

Eros is the romantic kind of love. It's the love you have for your spouse or fiancé. The Greek word "eros" is translated to mean a passionate or romantic love. It's also translated to mean a sexual love. Eros love is very important in marriage. This is the one type of love that does not appear in the Bible.

Storge is the love that you have for your parents, siblings, children, and other members of your family. This is the type of love that exists between parents and their children. This is also the type of love that should exist among Christians.

Be kindly affectionate to one another with

brotherly love, in honor giving preference
to one another;
Romans 12:10
New King James Version (NKJV)

A new commandment I give to you, that
you love one another; as I have loved you,
that you also love one another. By this
all will know that you are My disciples,
if you have love for one another.
John 13:34-35
New King James Version (NKJV)

Love is an action. It's a commitment. In this renewed and rekindled relationship with God, commit yourself to spending time with Him by setting aside time for Him each day, praying, and talking to Him, and reading and studying the Bible.

Prior to distancing yourself from your relationship with God, what kind of love where you showing God?

Do you realize how much God loves you? How do you know?

How can you show God that you love Him?

Prayer:

Father God teach me how to love. Teach me how to truly love You and how to love others. I now realize just how much You truly love me. You've shown me that through Your actions and commitment to me. I want to show You how much I love You through my actions and having a deeper commitment to You and Your Word. Forgive me for not loving You as I should have in the past. I do truly love You God and pray my actions from this day forward will show You just how much I love You. This I pray in Jesus' name. Amen.

DAY FOURTEEN

Reunited

Congratulations! You've reached Day 14, the last day of this devotional. By today, you should have been able to implement the steps from the previous days and started to rekindle your relationship with God.

To reunite with someone is defined as you come together again with that person after a period of separation. Prior to reading this devotional, you may have been separated from God for a period of time. Something happened where it made you distance yourself from Him and your relationship with Him. Prayerfully, after going through the days of this devotional, you've gotten some tools and information to rekindle the flame in your relationship with God.

In Day 1, you came to the conclusion that your relationship with God wasn't what it was before. You realized that something had gone wrong with the relationship. In Day 2, you evaluated when things started to turn in your relationship and dedication to your relationship with God. In Day 3, you were able to identify what that "something" was that put a wedge between you and God. You needed to identify it if you were going to be able to rekindle your relationship with God. In Day 4, you realized that although you may have walked away from God, He never left you. He remained right there beside you. In Day 5, you asked God for forgiveness and repented of any sin you committed as a result of being mad or upset with God.

In Day 6 and Day 7, you learned what it really meant to have an intimate relationship with God and what intimacy really was. In Day 8, you were encouraged to have that unpleasant conversation with God where you told Him how you were feeling – if you were mad or upset with Him – and why you were feeling that way. In Day 9, you learned the cautiousness of being angry with God. In Day 10, you were encouraged to forgive yourself for how your relationship with God had went before when you distanced yourself away from Him. In Day 11, you were able to identify some "thieves" that may have rob you of time where you kept putting spending time with God off. In Day 12, you learned about going to God in prayer. In Day 13, you learned that God's love for you remained. You also learned about the four types of Biblical love.

Now you find yourself on Day 14 of the devotional. On this day, I want you to celebrate that you realized your relationship with God was questionable or not as it should be and you've implemented the steps to rekindle it and get it back on track. Today is a day of celebration! Rejoice in the fact that you have reunited yourself with God in an intimate relationship. What once seemed lost is now found. No matter how long you distanced yourself, God was right there waiting to welcome you back into relationship with Him. He missed you and was overjoyed that you rekindled your relationship with Him. So, take Day 14 to rejoice at what's to come as you walk with God and talk with God daily. God has so much in store for you and as you walk with Him and talk with Him, He will reveal all that He has for you. He will guide you and order your steps in the path that He has for you. You wondered if He remembered you. Yes, He does!

What have you learned during these 14 days?

What will you do differently now that you didn't before concerning your relationship with God?

Which day of the devotional really spoke to you? Why?

**For the prayer for today, my challenge to you is that you construct a heartfelt prayer to pray to God.

LaKecia Wilson

LaKecia Wilson is a prophetic leader operating under her God given mandate of *Isaiah 43:8, "Bring out the people who have eyes but are blind, who have ears but are deaf."* LaKecia embraces her assignment from God by empowering and pointing people toward their destiny and purpose in God, and helping them reach their greatest potential to do the work God has called them to. She operates in her gifts both within the Church and in marketplace ministry to help others soar to greater heights for the Kingdom. LaKecia is the author of two other books, *Singled Out for Success: God Has Chosen You"* and *"If I Get Left Behind: Surviving in Post Rapture Times."* LaKecia resides in Illinois with her husband, Bennie.

www.ingramcontent.com/pod-product-compliance
Lightning Source LLC
Chambersburg PA
CBHW051430090426
42737CB00014B/2908